Tacoma Narrows

Tacoma Narrows

Mitchell Parry

GOOSE LANE

Edited by Sue Sinclair.
Cover illustration by Creatas Images.
Author photo by Julia Kenyon.
Cover design by Lisa Rousseau.
Book design by Julie Scriver.
Printed in Canada.
10 9 8 7 6 5 4 3 2 1

Library and Archives Canada Cataloguing in Publication
Parry, Mitch, 1960-
Tacoma Narrows / Mitchell Parry.
Poems.
ISBN 0-86492-450-X
I. Title.
PS8631.A77T33 2006   C811'.6   C2005-906435-8

Published with the support of the Canada Council for the Arts and the New Brunswick Culture and Sport Secretariat. We acknowledge the financial support of the Government of Canada through the Book Publishing Industry Development Program (BPDIP) for our publishing activities.

Goose Lane Editions
469 King Street
Fredericton, New Brunswick
CANADA E3B 1E5
www.gooselane.com

For Marlene

Table of Contents

Faithless

Burn Unit

Tacoma Narrows

Faithless

Night Wind

Something is running in the wind
tonight: nocturnal longing, raven, ghosts,
I don't know. In the next room
a woman's voice opens,
I think of you.

Outside my window an elk steps,
bends & nibbles. Her valentine rump,
that mouth, the heartbreak of her ankles. In the distance
men's shouting fights the wind
& loses. She ignores them, moves from one blade
of grass to the next.

Come closer: I need to whisper this:
this is what it is to be human
& in love. The body pulling itself forward,
perfect, toward all the things it needs; desire
facing down the wind, the darkness,

all threats, shouts & silences until the last.

On Sparrow Song
— for Rosana

i Argument

Call it song, this quarrelsome chatter raining
from the balcony, wire-legged staccato
puncturing what silence the city can give. It speaks
to the green world beyond our concrete. Your own voice
wants to dance this way, wants a body that soft
& abrupt & puffed up against the cold. Imitation

is all you can hope for. To mimic sparrow's chirp,
pucker up: the wind has come begging.

ii Fly

Sometime in 1969, Nick Drake manages to pull himself from
despair long enough to pick up his guitar and record "Fly." The
song is short — just over three minutes — but it stands alone.
He's hidden from his depression by running to his parents'
house in Tamworth-in-Arden. In just over five years he will be
dead of an overdose. Tryptizol: popped like aspirin whenever he
needed it. But listen:

it's a warm day, warm enough for an open
window. Hear how his voice rises, how he lets
that opening call, *Please*, break

under its own weight? How he finally lifts song
above a speaking voice, his mouth to your ear.
But when he sings the word *recompense*,

he starts to smile. You might think
it's the word, maybe it's the open window. I believe the smile
looks out on the garden, the sparrow

singing with him. Notes spin like clockwork,
the insistent long-dead sparrow answering the guitar strings
tinny and brittle under his fingers, and shouting *Here I am*

Here I am for all time.

iii Verglas

The first day you could still
hear them, chuckling
& bickering & tut-tutting
in the shrubs. At night
ice weighed down the bush, sealed it
like a jar in a cold basement. A mind
full of natter. But as time went on,
what struck you hardest was the absence
of birds, their songs & the soft hyphen
of flight muffled by freezing rain.

                              Branches split
& shattered on the pavement. Days gleamed.
We listened for the tell-tale creak as trees calved
new catastrophes, crushed cars, broke windows.

By then, the sparrows were utterly silent.
How many survived only to emerge
& find their architecture
demolished, split trees already
making their glacial progress towards death. Fluffed
throats beating and no nest to roost in. What
would we call that first song?
When thaw came branches shrugged

off ice. Gleaming rods
cascaded to the pavement, quick casts of branch
& twig. We ran our fingers along them, thinking,
This is how rain feels. This
is where a sparrow stood.

iv Parlez-moi d'amour

You remind me that the Virgin Mary
is a sparrow — for her bright eyes
perhaps. Or her grace. I prefer
Edith Piaf, her small buckled shoes,
a voice warbling from centre stage,
regretting nothing. Remember

the music box we bought by the Seine? We sat on a bench
in the Tuilleries & cranked "Parlez-moi d'amour"
to the sparrows hawking your hands for bread. (I cannot
slice baguettes now without drawing blood). On your back

is a tattoo I paid for. Le moineau. *I like pain*,
you told the man who needled it into your skin. This is my gift
to you: a sparrow who will fade
slowly over the years but never fly
away. Singing what all gifts sing: *Here.*

I am.

Self Taught

First remove that tyrant, I.
No plucking, no coddling — no time
for gentleness. Knock it out,
chip free the stubborn tooth
(you are not the first person
to do this). Do not grin blood. No one wants to hear
about your lost loves, your abandoned family.
Gutter them.
                Outside there is weather.
Name it: snow. Not sweeping, not
curling around the lamps. Stop. Leave it:
this snow *falls*. Two cats fight
under a balcony, roll in the snow
and wail with grief. One pins
the other to cold ground, cuffs and bites
and struts into night. His high tail
is his own song. The loser vanishes.
Go outside and find him — under a car,
hiding in the woods, it doesn't matter.
Sing to him (this is imperative). Coax him
with songs of nonsense or loss (it doesn't matter).
When he comes to you, look at the ache
in his eyes. Name it.

Imperfect Sonnet

Gray declares its walls extremely thin.
Sinus venosus — hollow of the veins, but also
hollow of the heart. This much I half-know
from college Latin, the *Anatomy*. My doctor's in

an architectural mood: the problem is my atrium,
its contractions are completely wrong,
stammering and interrupting the ventricle's song
with clumsy rhythm: *ba-dum, ba* — , *ba-dum,*

ba — . *Learn to live with it,* he says. *Your heart
is healthy otherwise.* But how? Each night
its clopping beat drags me from sleep with a start
my lover cannot soothe. The dream: a faceless man
taps at my window & shines a light
I have to turn away from — it is that bright.

Perilous Breathing

Scudded crow, tatters
against sky, wings useless today. Full mouth
cries out its shredded *awe awe*, strained flights
then air's rebuttal.
      On still days herons sail
above the marsh. Waiting
is our only motion, the cicada hum
of pause. But
this gust shouts, *Action!*
Hurls scavengers to leaves,
leaves to concrete & only concrete
left untouched. Wind alone
can sing itself: your song chokes
on its own
too patient breathing.

Perilous breathing: *septum,*
the doctors tell you, spongy
aileron, breath's rudder: How it
deviates at the angle of suffocation,
says *no way* to sudden gusts & leaves you
floundering.
                 The fish
in you. Murky ancient wriggle
tugs you benthic to dry land. Greet
wind's sudden face:
it hooks you, carp-mouthed.
Drowning in surfeit
of air, o gasp-eyed mullet,
you cannot
                breathe
to breathe.

     ◉

This breath:
               or this — . Could be
all.

     ◉

Said plainly:
when the wind blows
you can't breathe.
Little world, your mouth
an equator, drifted north. Spin
your own coriolis, twirling with earth's
twirling, pilotless
in time's wake. Air pools
on your cheeks, purls
around nostril & mouth & will
not go in.

And yet you love wind,
who gives and takes away.
Hurricane, breeze, rage of sudden
gusts — love it to the bone.
Because its song is fingers
squeaking on frets, is flight,
is song, is the breath
we are born to lose.
Catch it.

That Night the Wind Ploughed

The body bristles. Anger like that night the wind ploughed fists
of snow against the walls. Like being at sea, we said: spume and
crash, rock pools flushed and flushed. The house cocooned in
snow, must have been miles thick and still unable to muffle the
wind.

Marooned in the bedroom, it was only natural the hull should
breach, cascades of glass and snow rushing onto my bed. Joy
or terror (both) — we screamed while the room turned into a
twisted Xmas card, drifts forming on the blankets, curtains catch-
ing the snow like cedar boughs.

Mum hid the storm and shattered calm behind a towel and card-
board, then punished us for the wind and our screams.

The official story says this never happened: next day I traced the
most precise crack in the remaining pane, sliced my finger along
the fault line.

Boozehound

is a bloodhound. He's in your father's
limp embrace & mumbled confessions
of love, your mother's long nights flushing
pills down the toilet. He's the blurry ghost
dog in old photos, the one who taught you to roll over
& show your belly when threatened, how to growl
or wag. Hear how his slack-throated
high lonesome blues curve into the night, moon
or no moon, the mournful jubilation of his baying.
Don't pretend you don't recognize him: he's been on your trail
for years, over all fences & through every stream:
none of the old tricks will work.
Whose screen door bangs the neighbours awake
all night? Who bought the winning ticket
and used it for rolling? Who always says
just one more & means just *more*?
You're going to have

to tame him. Look into those sad-sack
red-rimmed eyes & stare him down,
remind him who's boss.
Say, *heel*.
Say, *sit*.
Stay.

Vacaciones Perdidas

In the flat cold of a Spanish winter
it's easy to believe in long western plains,
whirlwinds of snow in headlights
on the way home. But then clatter
drifts from steamed windows of *cervecerias*
& at the foot of the cathedral
Catalans dance the *sardana*
like white birds weaving the floodlit spires.
Tight rings circle just so,
raising hands & sweat in unison.

And we are in love with what is not ours.
Our holiday has been spent pulling cigarettes
from the gutters we scoured for lost change,
galleries seen from the park & long nights
not spent over coffee or *tapas*.
                              Down
& out, they used to call it. Nostalgia.
How longing leads us to men & women
gleaming in the cold. Each gesture tells us
This is how it's done. As if
it were that easy — circles bobbing, breaking only
to include another dancer in the halo of breath,
all arms raised to shout
home.

Elegy for Two Greek Kittens

Mid-October.
Somewhere a piano repeats
near-chords, & on the other side
of town the kittens we saved
are closer to death.
                    Two went this morning —
an inaudible stammer in the rhythm of the day.
Somewhere I have a picture
of you, bleary & buried in kittens long before dawn,
fishbone claws struggling to tug the bottle
from your hand. Tonight the names
we never gave them are dry
between bared teeth.

                    To have come so far
following the faint scent of adventure
& failed reunions
only to find always,

always the wide pink mouth of need
crying at dawn. Three weeks
of ringworm mewling shit & our best efforts
dying quickly & painfully as all
hopes & battered things die: open-mouthed,
abandoned.

Between Belgrade and Skopje

After the next mountain, another.

Near the city the train follows
a river the colour of eggplant.
One week into the war

passengers still smell immunity
in creosote and steel. This corridor to the South.
In a compartment the window splinters,
reticulates haystacks, the television tower. Stones,

the conductor says. In Thessaloniki
they bloom into shells and bullets; glass shards
pierce empty seats. In the heat
at the edge of a field a boy

with hair like grain braces himself,
thin arms stretched wide to catch
the train's passage, eyes tight against
the dust. Beaming.

Skopje

Around sunset the train wheezes into Skopje
and stops. A man in uniform
taps the wheels with a long-handled hammer.
The darkened station. Fifty miles behind us a woman in black

sits under a bridge, weeping into her hands.
A milk-pale calf staggers beside the tracks.
When did I lose faith in the familiar?
A blur of late summer poplars through glass.

Like this woman, in her apartment near the station.
How she turns on a lamp with a shade
the exact orange of the sky behind her, filling
her room with sunset. How only we can see

what she has created. The obscure code tapped
on the wheels, a whistle. Station lights hum on
and the train lurches into the dark.

Balance

— after a photo by Jin Me Yoon

She is poised forever between moments,
the vertical in a postcard landscape
of natural geometry meeting right behind
her eyes. Thousands of miles to stand
here, immobile, by a lake either freezing
or thawing, snow advancing or receding. This
is how silence looks, sung by John Denver.
If one more person walks between her
& the camera she knows she is going
to scream. In a fraction of a second
she will pull on her coat, rub her hands
together & think of circles, coils, the twist
of her mother's hair, will remember:
there are no corners in the sky.

Trust

— for Bronwen Wallace

It's the bend of her back I love,
the flash of pale but freckled waist when
she stoops to pull weeds from the ditch.
Down the highway a cat stretches on the south
shoulder, rabbit on the north, clamped to gravel
by the speed that hit them. I've been
doing ninety all day, London Ilderton
Exeter Birr and home, cattle and horses wheeling
past the windshield. In Mitchell
the cemetery leans into the haze like candlelight on film.
Even the careful rows are slipping away: hard to walk
without stepping on *Father Infant Daughter Beloved Wife*.
Chronology breaks as old stones pick up recent names.
End of the line.

Brambles reclaim pasture, a collapsed
farmhouse, sunken coop. Like that
shredded windmill in the field ahead,
the one grown green with vines, gone
before I can find it in the rear-view and lost
by August. Or this woman by the highway,
turning her back to the hiss of speed, hoping
all that matters is the weed, the length
of her arm. Forgetting how much she has to trust us.

Distance

The station's signing off. Just time
for the news & national forecasts.
Up the band Ginsberg chants long lines about failure.

All day the sky was stretched
high & thin, blue
on blue on blue, further than blue
could reach. Night is startled & dry, air
wrung out after thick wet weeks.

This summer
what I learned was the love of bones. Shin bones,
cheekbones, collarbones, oh shoulder
blades, femora, sterna (heart's
flimsy breastplate), knuckles, knees.
Not scars or bruises but
brittle & persistent memories,
smoothed & grooved by tendon, by muscle.
Personal histories in pouches of flesh
shaping how we are around what we've been through.

Tomorrow will toss you far west, over mountains
abrupt and perfect as a spine.
What we must never forget are bones long
as evening shadows,
thin stalks wading in shallows,
desire, a promise kept.

Ragged Hymns — While You Were Away

A bird is lost in the dark.
Its panic drags me to the porch.
Moths buzz like paper against the bulb, wheel off
to sulk, scorched and bewildered. All week
the cat has plucked starlings
from the lawn, pigeons from the eavestrough.
Tonight sleep would be like glass: brittle,
splintered. The lost bird circles
above the house, voice breaking against the unfamiliar sky.
In his dreams, cat crouches and bristles.
Springs. If he still had a tail it would lash
like tides coursing after the moon.

What have I made of this summer without you?
Severed wings on the curb,
naked hatchlings purpled and bulging in the sun.
In all places where your mouth shaped air there is silence.
All songs are ragged hymns tossed
into black water from the stern.
Nearer my God.

Listen: there is no flight —
only falling endlessly deferred. Stumbling open-armed
is not longing, is stumbling only. All I know of desire
cannot extend beyond this bare bulb, spirals of dust
and smoke. A bird lost in the night,
hoping song can light its way home.

Telling

Grey city, chill air, the promise of snow, the promise
& still no snow. November wind
blows the dead end of summer
up: birch leaves fly onto the balcony.
Rind of the year,
chaff. What the cat dragged in.
Gutters are clotted
with leaf mulch, slick & brown
& rotten. Treacherous. Bicycle
tires slip; the heart clutches. That risk. I sip

and turn back to the dark corners
of our darkening home. Abandoned dishes,
mugs used as ashtrays, the cat dragging
himself from room to room, complaining. Can we invent
a better name for betrayal? Whiskey helps,
though not enough. You worry
over every detail. My hand on your shoulder
could set your bones free, bring you
the ease you need for sleep. Or fog
the window.   I want

one day like water: cool, yes, & so clear
only the weight of the glass tells me that it is full.

Faithless

I can never tell you this.
Nearly winter, which means nothing
can make up its mind. That first

separation: we agree to meet
& talk & grieve. The bus I ride
over the mountain stops

at the lookout. A bride & groom
get on, giggling, sit together
in the driver's seat. I stare

at the paint-brush ponytail
of the woman in front of me.
The photographer tells the bride to kiss

the driver. *Don't cheat on me
already*, the groom laughs. The city
stretches on & on below,

a white limousine, roses, cars & couples
parked side by side. The newlyweds thank us
for this gift we have received. Bonne chance,

a woman shouts after them, as if
that were enough. I will never
tell you this story: how irony & pain

embrace, walk hand in hand.
How the bride wore the high-heeled
sneakers you wanted. This is the wrong stop

but I get off anyway. For the length
of the bus my wedding band rings
against each pole meant to keep me upright.

Letters to a Brief Wife of Ten Years

First of October, our month, & it's still
summer. My neighbour scrapes rust

from the fire escape, paints it
Brazilian yellow & green. In the yard

chestnuts are splitting. Squirrel
spins one in her hands, skins it

in tight green spirals. A concert nearby
rolls in the air, the PA clotting

the alleys with sound. You've moved
to this neighbourhood, but we won't

meet. Listen: the singer drowns out
the band, spurts lyrics into echo. We

won't meet. If your windows
face west, you can hear this, too.

᠀

Faust on the radio, same weight
as this grey sky. I've only had

one dream of flight, & that
enough: an old woman tells me that to fly

I need only remember to fly. Then lift —
no wires, no mirrors, no hands. Ten,

fifty miles up into blizzard. I was supposed
to be watching you. Always. Distracted,

I could see our whole world, its Escher
buildings, minarets, staircases leading

nowhere. Only remember to fly. In the dream,
I thought of birds, their eyes, the lure

of fluffed throats. Imagined rising in the arch
of another's wings, my heart

pressed tight between the shoulders of
the heron's heart. Around sunset

a ribbon of sky unfurls on the horizon,
promises cold, promises night, promises morning.

Suddenly, late summer. Lobelia pouring
through the cracks in the driveway. You'd like them,

small ear tufts, the blue & yellow hearts
almost electric. Stems green as our old cat's

eyes welcoming us home. She's gone now,
though I keep the bed she died on. I tried

to press the flower in a notebook for you
but it slid out, it's gone, you're gone

& all the things we tried to make.
On our anniversary posters sprouted

on the lamp posts: lost cat. His name
is Solomon, he's young & on his own. Not

as wise as his namesake, or wiser
for choosing to leave. I know you'd have found him,

calling his name from street
to street, under bushes — you wouldn't rest

until you heard his answer, your heart always
big enough for lost causes. Forgive me:

I'm still learning to let lost things stay lost.
Hours & days. The flowers come & go

once a year. The dictionary tells me they like
shade & sun, can thrive in both. Much love.

Burn Unit

Burn Unit
— after a photo by Raphael Gaillarde

Palms in the atrium murmur
the comfort of warmth, sunlight
through sloped glass. She must

remind herself of this — how light
falls, or hurtles at the speed of itself
to open eyes. Under such astonishing

fronds she could wait out any storm, runnels
streaming overhead. Water purling
on thick leaf. Frog chorus. She needs

this, to remember. Yes:
how heat should feel: clear and green,
overarching. Horizontal.

No. Take it back. You know nothing,
have never taken the long
forced march to Dickinson's hour

of lead after great pain. All you have
is a photograph: three men in masks and gloves
carry a woman from the bath. Head and shoulders,

torso, legs and feet. She lies across
their chests, cradled in their elbows. The one
who holds her shoulders

is out of step. They have come from the bath,
where her skin was washed with the care
we lavish on the dead. Or those who've returned

from the edge and can tell us nothing. Dousing the flames
brings not the end of pain but a change
in pitch, the body seared,

in time, scarred. For now, fresh gauze
and cleaned burns can only be entrusted
to hands, to arms. A stretcher is too rough.

And so they carry her. She allows herself
to be carried. The camera holds
the group in place. The shutter

clicks. For this moment
she is translated into silver, is light,
is carried: weightless.

Behind them the hospital corridor
stretches antiseptic, terminal, a scene
from an airport: arrivals, departures, departures.

&

The woman wrapped in gauze. Before she burned,
what colour was orange, was yellow? Did she flinch
from light? What was pain, how much

was too much, back when she waded
through air, before air ignited and fed
the heat that fed on her? What name

can we give those days? Now she rides the hours
from one nerve to the next. She knows
she will never be as before.

Stay with the photograph.
That, and the caption, an interview with the man
whose arms support her hips. He likes the photo,

he says, *because it shows how everybody*
carries the sick in his arms. What is the opposite
of burden? Trusting herself to their hands,

she raises them all back into muscle, blood,
the intricate grace of walking. And the heart, its need
to open. The one in the middle knows this,

says, *If you get used to people's suffering, it's best*
to change professions. Three masked men carry
a woman in their arms. The shortest out of step.

In the end, it's the body
we come back to — rags, bones,
flesh. Picture her rising from the tub,

held up, supported by water's
buoyancy. When they lift her
she sinks

back into herself. She knows
this is a kind of love, these hands that
wrap her with a tenderness difficult

to bear. But then the lift, the tug
of her body back into the strange gravity
she occupies. Pain, ease, sleep,

pain: all old meanings gone
in a flash.

✍

A bandaged woman. Three men carry her. One hooks
his hands around her calves. The one who speaks
cradles her hips, gloved hands concealing the gauzed cleft

of buttocks. This could all collapse,
but doesn't. The one out of step turns
his body to hers, holds her heart

to his heart. So like a dance — unable to see
past her shoulder, he trusts the others
to lead, looks into her face through

his mask, her gauze. Speaks to her, to the fear
in her eyes. The fingers of his right hand
arch back, away, as though guiding

something infinitely fragile. Dandelion,
dust motes. Light. Love: he does not hold her up:
he holds her *to him* with his palms.

Sang d'encre

All through that winter, the tree outside
cracked & shivered, its heart splitting
& splitting, over & over under
the weight of ice. The *verglas*:

how it killed something in us: trust,
certainty. The sparrows hiding inside
the heart. This year the tree is
dead, its branches black
filigree reticulating grey sky. Knots
& knuckles. Wet twigs. Today

I bought myself a fountain pen, black
& gold. A bottle of ink. I wrote
to you & thought of jet, its polish.
I read once that negative space
cannot exist until the first line
is drawn to define it. Here it is: this
is how the heart looks when it decides
to give up.

Put on a white dress. Something
cotton, faded & soft. I want to dance with you
before first snowfall, while the grass is still pale green
beneath our feet.

How the world changes, or the heart. Yesterday
the maple outside your window was just
tree, or cross-hatching at best, scritch-scratch

of ink. Winter solstice today, full moon tonight.
Around sunset, you remember
that what you will miss most when you die

is this light, windows at the college & the cemetery
pulsing red. How every detail stands
in relief: each brick, the slow-geyser jets

of poplar behind a wrought-iron fence.
The fence protecting the orderly dead, marble
headstones glowing. From this point on

the days reach longer & longer. Not *sang d'encre*
but *l'encre du sang*: light brings you back,
as always, to the body. The maple glows pink

& you can almost imagine it capillaries,
veins. Flesh is light, is sky
offered up by the long arms of branches.

Cross Country

Two days north of Montreal, the woman
beside me starts speaking Spanish. *Muy bonito,*

we agree, the *paisaje nuevo* swinging past
bus windows. New land. The highway

sweeps her to husband,
me to you. She tells me we are both

travelling on faith & I remember how
our thighs brushed as we jostled in sleep,

her head lolling onto my shoulder. The woman
across the aisle is from Osaka. At night

she wets her face with a damp cloth,
rubs in lotion & folds herself perfectly

into the two seats. In the morning she plucks
her eyebrows, drops each hair into a paper

sack before moving on to the next. Did I
love her stranger's precision? Last night I rode

beside a man with bad teeth & a litany of failures —
sinuses, back, knees. No work.

He entrusted them to me, these relics.
For some reason I tapped

his knee & we agreed that he would be
all right. Quick-forged friendships:

next time we'll go fishing, he said, knowing
that we won't. I phone you

from every station of my crossing. *Love.*
Don't worry. Sudbury, Thunder Bay,

Regina. We negotiate, confess the fear
behind our voices. *Don't worry.* Telling each loop

in each flex-cord that unites us. Worrying.
Calgary, Banff, Kamloops. A friend reminds me

this is a leap year. I'm mid-jump. This time
tomorrow I'll turn to find you naked, watching me

from the doorway & all the time zones
I've passed through will funnel into *now*,

& now. How the articles of love are always
indefinite & present, imperfect.

Early Autumn

We could never mistake this light for another —
too thin & yellow for warmth. Behind you
the trees are turning, speaking only of endings.
A sparse column of midges spirals loosely
above the ground, collapses into circling pairs.

You drowning in dull sunlight. All week the maples
have been scattering loss's red & gold in the street
while you stared into the grey distance
of your pain. Following the death drawing you
deeper into your body, the cumulous blossoms
of tumour.

In time this air will bite. Starlings will cluster
on steaming chimneys while those of us who remain
will follow the sun from room to room. Light, trees, cold.
I want to say your dying makes these meaningless,
but O the sun, the turning, you.

Ghazal XXXIX
— "John Thompson, The End"

How the lungs fill the moment
after something has passed. Look: heron.

Staggering home at night, I want
to sleep in the snow. Stars cling to my lashes,

the open gate. Iron peeling. Maple
flings itself upward, grapples with grey sky.

The house burns, the barn burns, all poor
animals. Come morning, scratch for relics.

Pissed to the split rafters of the heart,
he tilts his shotgun at the clock's moon face.

Scratch your last lines on a napkin, grind
it under heel. Satisfied?

Something has passed. Nature abhors
nothing. How silence echoes.

If you sit, I will drink with you. Let me
pour. A table round enough for all.

Het Puttertje

The bird's name means drawer of water.
A tether links his ankle to the wall.
Resilience in this northern sun — the goldfinch amazingly
raises his chained cup as though drawing from a well, tilts
back his head & pours beakfuls over thirsty song. This
is his strength, to know God marks his fall.

At thirty-two Carel Fabritius has seen one family plucked
by death, has abandoned Amsterdam & Rembrandt for
remarriage & Delft. Later this year his body
will be shattered by explosion. His second wife
will spend the rest of her days seeking his pieces
in drains, between paving stones, finding
his powdered bones glazing stuccoed walls
flaking & yellow on quiet afternoons. Today
he paints this sparrow in motley whose flight
occurs only in the precision of his hand & eye.
The goldfinch eyes him coolly, pins him to immobility:
I know who you are. Fabritius shivers,
dips a brush. Paints fine ankles, fine chain.
A parched yellow wall.

Waiting

Look at the way your hands move,
spastic, not-quite-uncertain,

the songs they try to cull
from the air. You've had too much

to drink & the whole world knows it. Crows
complaining about something outside. Failure.

Where is your wife? The children
you vowed never to have? The woman

you love curls into sleep, her hips
pressing into another man, his years-old love.

Someone sings *Lieder* on the radio, stops;
the audience pauses long before applause. There is

a poem in this, but this isn't the poem. This
is about bottoming out, about dried

rain barrels & washed-out roads in Turkey, the next-
to-last drink, the friend who jabs a finger into

your ribs & says, *No way*. A continent
from home you wait for the ferry, the bus,

morning. Other side of dawn you spill
into her arms on the dock, the woman of your dreams

at the time. Crows complain their years-old
love. The audience pauses.

Drunk, with Axe

Give the city boy his whiskey. Send him
to the woodshed with a ten-pound
maul & an axe. Let there be light rain,
drizzle, slick paths & moss. A round
of cedar, its wet heart whorled
on the chopping block. Give him that, & time:

this is how he wants to prove a man.

Give the man an axe, a maul, a grudge
& whisky. Give him everything
you've got — he can take it
or leave it. He wants you to see he can
be wild, bush-Byron, dangerous. Lubricate
the world the way he's greased himself:
rain, moss, wet wood.

Watch him swing the axe & miss. *Strike one.*

Last fall, machete, wasp nest in the brambles. Bad aim.
Kitchen knives know the taste of his thumbs.
He's been known to mistake chickens for children,
umbrellas for deer. Armchair naturalist. All that holds his blood
from the world is a fabric even paper can cut.

He drops the axe & reaches for
the maul, tries the heft of the word, imagines himself
grizzly, cougar. The image doesn't take. When he swings
it over his head, the weight pulls him
backward.

                    Inside
the house a woman feeds
the wood stove, plucks at her sweater
& listens for the missed blow, axe thud,
the five-toes-left-behind scream. She thinks
tourniquet, antiseptic, gauze. The blue sheets
torn up for bandages. She makes room
in the freezer. Because you never know.
                                        But he's
still out there, the stupid fucker, head
full of fumes & Trakl & other clichés. The cedar round
is a disgrace — sliced & bruised but otherwise
intact. He's butchering it, he's too drunk
to care. He arcs the maul
above his head.
                    You know
where this is going, don't you? I thought
I did, too — can there be a poem
without blood? What if he goes inside, leaves
the wood for tomorrow, swears off hooch & takes up
yoga? What if he kisses the woman, dances her socks off
& sets the table for dinner?

                    On the other hand,
last year dozens of people were injured by placemats.

St. Pat's

Hurley's Irish Pub, St. Patrick's Day, & all
the old anthems on the speakers. *Say it ain't so.*
Spirit in the sky. I'm drunk

on beer (not green, thank all the saints), in love
with a woman not my wife. Sunlight
peering through the window behind me, creeping

across the table, the room. *I'm on my way
from misery.* Van Morrison's "High Summer."
Three suits are hitting on the blonde waitress

with the Celtic tattoo. The salesman grabs
her arms, squeezes, says *Listen
to this.* Dishes crash in the kitchen.

I'm looking for something holy in all this. I think
it's there, but I can't name it. The way
she steps into the sun as she eases

herself free, how her laughter opens
the room, her earrings flashing when she spins
to the bar & leaves him unharmed,

basking in grace. I know,
I know: this isn't beauty, but it is. On the street

a luminous gull coasts down Crescent, turns left
at the intersection. Someone opens
the door of the Y at just the right moment, steps

into the sun. Nick Drake on a car radio,
Aznavour. How the woman behind me pronounces
plastique — twelve then thirteen pigeons

sunning on a tin roof.

Morning

We sit by the window, sharing
a cigarette. The blanket you are wrapped in
marries sky & earth, is the colour

of that blue stillness
herons carry into flight: how we ache
for the lifting of bones. What is the word

for this blue? More joyous & driven than
cerulean. The exact shade of blue
the snow assumes at evening. Remember

the deer we saw this morning, their eyes
bewildered by the snow, soft mouths
shovelling the leaves clear inch

by inch. We watched them eat, high-
stepping & then vanishing over the fence.
The line of cleft pocks will remain

until tomorrow or the next day. We turn
from the window, return to what needs
doing, while outside deer tracks freeze

solid. The body's love letter to itself, saying,
Come to me. I will wait.

Boxing Day, Corbett Road

Wood stove smokes the living room and I open
the door, follow the deck around to where the sun
still shines on the frost-rimed house. The uncut

grass gleams hay-blonde in the meadow. In the house
your husband's memories sing of blood, sing whiskey
and blades. Even the dog is exhausted. I tap

the fishbowl to break the ice
& there are only two survivors. A school
of starlings lifts off at once from the apple tree. Heron

croaks the length of the valley. He raises a roof
with his flight & his voice. Who knew love
could weigh so much? Juncoes in the clematis,

black-cowled like monks, monks
or hangmen. Look south:
deer tracks cut desire lines through the tall

meadow. We could follow them to the fence
& leap.

Hazelnut

Coastal winter, so it's either raining
or raining. Last night I woke up in a race, heart

shouting out the old cub scout oath: *DOB*
DOB DOB. Come morning we're still

uneasy, bruised & stiff from
wrestling with our dreams. Days

like this, eyes won't meet, we can only say *I want*
and *I know. Sorry*. We keep scuffing

each other's edges. I circle downtown, store
to store, but nothing is worth buying. Nothing

is worth anything much. Late afternoon
wrings itself out enough to coax an eagle

into slow useless loops over the city. Empty
hunting. The bus home passes courts, closes,

crescents, cul-de sacs, alleys — small streets
that loop back to nowhere. An injured gull

squawks & squawks; orange-bellied hawk yawns
on the hydro line. I want to say that being

is hard & cruel, but that's not right. Hunter
could easily be hunted. We do our best. Outside

our door the cat rears up, lunges against
my hand the way we lunge toward each other. Fiercely

hungry. Can our best be enough for now? Stop
on the way back, love. Look at that ridiculous tree,

poor contorted hazelnut. Its twists & loops, all
the perfect knots we follow to get to here.

Snowfall, Pender Island

In from the woodpile, hands
resin-browned & stitched with cedar
slivers. Feed the fire against a cold

so chill it grips the bones, says *We'll*
meet again later. The ridge talcumed
with snow, the treetops; in the valley

it's puddles, just slush. Early
spring. Clumps of snowdrops.
Crocus splash

on the field, bright purple with daring
yellow hearts. When they furl
into evening they'll be invisible, hands

folded, closed. Open yourself
in a hot bath, go out onto the deck
naked & steam the air. Look for deer:

no deer. No grouse, but you can hear them
in the lane of blackberries. Fox
you never see, except in restless

dreams. Pheasant once. You stopped
the truck & stared at the purple breast, that
strut-strut-strut. A doe once, too, outside

the bedroom window while you were making
love. You wanted your hands on her then,
the muscled pulse of her neck, could have

kissed that soft mouth. It made perfect sense
at the time: love & love & love. How we look
at what doesn't see us. Stop the truck, drive

on, stop the truck. Try not to stare. You want
to believe in eye-beams, strong cords tying us
to the things we see: crow-hollowed apples withered

on the branches, chicken scratch, dog
tracks. Eagle at the edge of the field, preening.

Goshawk

Her beauty hit us first & hardest,
which is to say we knew
that she was wild. What towhee

has always known. Goshawk
on the fencepost. We looked it up:
uncommon

to rare, the female is fierce
in defense, often attacks intruding
men. She fled when I approached,

but she was the intruder this time,
or felt it. We knew her by her blue-grey
back, the *rapid, steady wingbeats*

alternated with glide, by the weight
of her predation. Some mornings
I still can't believe we make it

through the night. We survive the fire
that never happened, the killer
not lurking in the attic. Wake

& feed the dog, feed the wood stove, warm
the home we're trying to claim & forget
that time plucks at our hearts saying,

Now, or *Now.* Owl pellets on the front
steps, the new lamb gone missing
from the next field. But did I mention

that she was beautiful, & wild? She's still
on the island, perched
high up, eating or hungry. Across the road

a mother calls her son's name.
Again. The dog wants his dinner,
wants his blanket, wants & wants. Feed the dog,

feed the fire & leave it roaring.
Leave the doors unlocked. We'll take off
our clothes, dance in woodsmoke in the yard,

singing, *Take me. Take me now.*

Birds, the names we give them
— for Sue Goyette

The power goes out & I remember
nothing. How fuses work, how
the body works, even the name of the bird

flicking millet from the feeder outside
my window. Some kind of finch,
I think, but that's the best I can offer. Too drab

for gold, too rosy for anything else & small
enough for a heartbeat. *Do you believe
in true love?* you ask, as if

there could be any other kind. I believe
in action: to true love, place it
level, make it ring. Birds, the names

we give them. Not names but verbs, perhaps. I swallow
joy, heron grief. To ring-necked pheasant
pride. To sparrow love.

Fourth Anniversary

and the last. Lisa Germano
on the stereo, "Paper Doll." A lawyer,
a desk, our particular version
of the old story. But also:

the day we married there were ospreys
fishing the river, herons, late summer
auroras. How could the omens
prove so wrong? Or right? What is this

in the taxonomy of years? Lead, paper,
tar, eggshells. Paper, I think — the ones
we signed, the ones you're served.
The lawyer says, *This will be easy.*

Love on the island, on the wing

Wake up to dawn chorus and the stammered flight
of wrens past the bedroom window. They'll hiccup
all day, rose trellis to Douglas fir and back. A male

hummingbird bullets straight up, then needle-loops
an elegant curve, the kazoo-trumpet fanfare and
bob-bob-bob of his swaggering dance. The female

keeps her nose buried in the fuschia, coquette
behind a fan. Then the jewel at his throat flashes
and she gasps, Oh my! They couple over

the pasture, above the stakes that mark where
the new house will be.
A man watches the shark-grey blue backs

of the swallows nesting under the deck where his wife
is potting tomatoes. A good home,
he thinks, this island. He wonders if wrens

ever pause outside their nest, ask,
How did I manage to get here? The woman goes
into the shaded kitchen for a glass of well water. He can

see her through the window, her throat as she drinks. When
she smiles the afternoon light falls
perfectly on her face. Oh my, he thinks. Oh my.

Insomnia

Can't sleep, can't sleep, the cedar shed
unbuilt, wood stove clicking down *hopeless*

hopeless. Words keep us in the past, & all
I've ever wanted has been words. Bird names, book

titles, the parts of my cat's face. The word for the feeling of
these clean pyjamas on my legs. That simple. There's want

and there's need: dog needs feeding, hens need water, shed
needs a roof. Last night I dreamt of murder across

the road & could only hide. How long
has this been going on? I came here — we all do — to learn

flesh & the size of the heart. Instead I think
mortgage, think *marriage, divorce*. Words — catches

in the throat, all that we have & crumpled paper
for all that. This morning wren made sounds at me,

meaningless & perfect.

After the Quake

I dropped to my knees & laughed
as the doorframe rocked above us: our hearts

flexing in aftershock. *I guess I should
put on some pants*, you said. As though nakedness

were barred from the Big One. I had expected
deep shifting, thunder, waves, a boatswain's roll

& sway — not muscled pounding like
Babe the Blue Ox humping the outside wall.

The animal earth trying to break in, the cyst
already pouched in your breast, my stammering

pulse — and the earth keeps shaking,
shifting. The weight of our arrival

sets the plates in motion. Some days
it shudders to remind us. False alarms

are the hardest gift, yanking from us
what we will only need once. The neighbours

gathered in the street, their faces glowing
torches against the unavoidable sun. How

their teeth rattled in their laughter: *I thought I was
a goner. The Lord walked through town*

this morning. Next time. Next time
we could hide our hands in that fur, ride

the lunges of its spine to Juan de Fuca
& up to our necks in ocean. What else can we do

but run into the living room, join hands, dance
a circle on the swaying floor, heel-toe, heel-toe.

Swan Song

The poems flow from the hand unbidden
and the hidden source is the watchful heart.
The sun rises in spite of everything
and the far cities are beautiful and bright.
　　　— Derek Mahon, "Everything Is Going to Be All Right"

My father died alone and sonless. No one
gathered to hear his last words, and he was too weak
to whisper anyway. Alive, I thought him spectral, foolish
knobby knees, hairs in his nose, the bad dancing
and the chipped enamel of his tenor voice. Easy
to forget in those last years that he had once ridden
penniless and unwashed across the ocean
to make the home he lost, and lost again. Love
in those we fail is simpler if we keep it hidden:
the poems flow from the hand unbidden;

crumbs for the birds change nothing. He drank himself
to tremors and the silence some lives offer
as the best course between anger and despair. Buried
in our genes, I think, someone will someday find
speculative maps of *Terra Incognita. Here*
be monsters. Here we stop and drink. The chart
pencilled in and passed on. What
did he say to the approaching dark? We nose into
the same stream when we arrive and when we depart,
and the hidden source is the watchful heart

that pulses memory through the gutters
of the blood. Some nights I try to drown myself
the way he did: whiskey by the bottle,
by the glass — it doesn't matter, so long as it
steers me out past midnight & the last lights
off my coast. A pose, I know: broken wing
of the sandpiper, swan song. Beautiful sadness is what I want
to call it, nobody loving failure like a drunk. At least
that's what I tell myself in the off-key shanty I sing.
But then *the sun rises in spite of everything,*

the bastard, as if this high-low romance were a missing
of the mark, a joke. I keep imagining myself kraken
stalking dark oceans, tugging every passing vessel to the depths
only to wake up in a wading pool with nothing real
to fear. What do I want to say, what do I ever say? In the end
I confess that I was wrong: there *is* flight,
great coasting rolls on high thermals, short bursts
from tree to tree. In failing, dear Dad,
you soared. The eastern sky has been embraced by night
and the far cities are beautiful & bright.

Campanology (Banff, Alberta)

Where the trail dips down toward small huts
Jay pauses & points. "Now *that's* bear shit." I'm glad
for the warning, but now the woods seem full
of shoulders, muzzles, claws. Five weeks
I've been studying bells — church bells,
chimes, warnings. Open mouths. Miracle bells:
St. Salaberga of Laon received a bell delivered
by a cow, rang it to protect her daughter
from the storms that haunted her. Or Anthony
of Egypt (not the Paduan saint of lost
things) chasing away demons with consecrated
peals, his pig wearing a dainty bell dangling
from an ear. In Greece once I drove to a village small
& empty enough that only the copper bells
of the goats told me the valley had inhabitants.
After Boris Godunov murdered Prince Dmitri the bell
that woke the town was exiled to sit tongueless
& frozen in Siberia. In this warmer climate I place
my trust in a small crotal, nutshell, & tie it to my pack,
knowing that for *dumb beasts which cannot pray the sound
of a consecrated bell is considered effective.* This is
my secular prayer, dear bruin — not a dinner bell
but a ringing warning. Take its sound
as announcing the outline of my presence in your
irrational, anonymous space. Let us both pass in peace.

How the Calendar Changes

First, the wind picks up to send
the old year away. You're inside, counting seeds

next to the wood stove, plotting next summer's
vegetables. I'm still out in the truck, rain pebbling

the roof and my caffeinated heart. The dog is at a loss:
he runs from house to truck, truck to house, shivering.

If I stare at the rain on the windshield I lose
the world; stare at the world and lose

the rain. I wanted to write about the stand
of arbutus on the south ridge — how their flesh

turns green when wet — but can't: we've been
arguing about this and that and but and but

and but. There's a new calendar over the kitchen
sink, next to the window overlooking the pasture

we'll build in, in time. Last year was photos of earth
from space; this year it's houses and villages, close up,

boats and cats. You line up leeks and onions, hot
peppers, arugula and mustard greens. What kind

of thing is a life? I don't know
how to stay angry. In a minute I'll leave

the truck and the rain, lead the wagging dog to the house
and towel him dry. He'll take up the couch. My arm

might brush your shoulder as I pass. Later,
we'll kiss in front of a picture of a door

in France, flower boxes, all the days ahead
arranged as though each follows

the next. For now, I'm still outside. Rain,
or the world. I know which I choose.

Moon Jelly

January on the coast & the dog's nose
slips out of hibernation. He puffs
his cheeks, gulps in ocean, beach, the crushed
and emptied crab shells. A murder of crows

stands at the water's edge, where small rocks
roll with the waves. The crows peck at the water
but won't get their feet wet. At the dog's approach
they levitate, noiseless for once, and settle

in the firs. Where they were, a moon jelly
pulses like a transparent heart, fist-sized,
against the incoming tide. Dog ignores it, head
full of crow scent, sea scent, faint flavour

of rot. He minds his business, pisses
on beached stumps too dense and waterlogged
to float away. The crows keep their distance,
eyes on the foamline. They can wait. They will.

The Explosion

My father told us
about the guy who got caught
in the boiler
(there were always accidents)
and when they pulled out the body
his head was the size
of a prizewinning pumpkin
(same colour too).

And things were always going off
before they were supposed to,
and every year someone lost a finger
to the meat grinder (and whoever got
that particular sausage
would never even taste
the difference).

Dad worked in the boiler room
and he was secretly proud
to work with machines
instead of with pigs
and Herefords (killing he couldn't do
and he hated to see the Italian men
moving in to remove the udders
and hooves after it was over
but before the shudders had stopped).

One day the greasy steel cylinder he loved
flew into a rage
and when the argument was over
they found him
clutching the pressure gauge.

Mum and I saw him in the hospital:
I remember two pale blue buttons
pleading from a mountain of blisters
and wet gauze.

And later (much),
my mother:

> *He was all blisters*
> *and scabs*
> *and he said he wanted me to*
> *(shudder)*
> *touch him under the sheet.*

After He Died

Dilation was the only word she could think of to describe it, the way it had felt in the beginning. Opening and opening, she couldn't stop it even if she'd tried. Days she spent brimming over and still it all rushed in — flowers, yes, and music, but also street lamps, the smell of snow in the air, long afternoon shadows and the certainty of early mornings. Knots in pine, fine gold chains, cracked photographs of distant ancestors, more flowers. Sunday afternoons spent listening to water dripping in the sink or the sound of her finger tracing the patterns on apple skin. How could she explain this need to touch all the things she needed, the way the world rushed into her even while she slept? Eggshells, fir needles and hand stitching, oh and hands themselves: half moons etched on finger joints and knuckles; the tributaries and hairs coursing along their backs; their ability to close. Close and open.

Tacoma Narrows

Tacoma Narrows

*I am an old man now, and when I die and go to Heaven there
are two matters on which I hope for enlightenment. One is
quantum electrodynamics, and the other is the turbulent motion
of fluids. And about the former I am really rather optimistic.*
— Horace Lamb

The day my father died the sky
should have been mammatus pouched.
Instability in the downward direction,

promise of heavy weather. The inside
of a thick pilled sweater. My love and I
ate toast and jam, chipotle, yellow-hearted

eggs in a room too warm. The dog
sighed on a rug, gave himself up
to the sun. Still air. Windows open

on mid-summer, warm and heavy. The buzz
and blur outside stopped long enough
to show us the red gorget of a rufous

hummingbird: hovering by the muntin-bars
it kept returning to, hoping at last
for the hymn-book red flower it knew them

to be. Little bullet, a thousand beats
of his barley heart, sweet pea brain
saying *go go go*. He waited for the light

and the sound of his passage to
catch up with him, long enough
to see us clutch our breath

before he burred off above the pasture. Burning
gleam of red at his throat, the quick glance
through the screen. I said, *I know that look.*

✦

Some nights my heart
won't let me sleep. It flops and jumps
and throws me out of bed, lights on and burning

until dawn. My doctor says it's just
an extra beat, mis-timing, stammer
in the circuit of the blood. Is faith in medicine

ever enough? My lover sinks —
no, tumbles — into sleep behind me, her arm
across my waist heavier and heavier until

the final letting go when she unspools. I stay on
in the dark, stretched between this side
of sleep and the next, eyes closed, the irregular

current of my pulse a squelching in my ear.
I can almost sleep, then think of old footage
from Tacoma, and the world drops out beneath me.

✦

In 1940, people crossed the country for the rough-
and-tumble thrill of Galloping Gertie,
Washington's roller-coaster bridge. Even

mountains shrank next to the marvels
of engineering. Suspension: the bridge
held itself above the swift-current swirl

of Tacoma Narrows by the confidence
of its own weight, one steady
pull against another, balance

of opposing forces, tug
of war. Deflection spread
the shear and bend to cables gripping

the flexible deck. Three thousand feet of gentle
swell, harmless vertical roll, a bolt of grey
satin rippling so elegantly above the water

that a camera was placed to film its slightest shrug.

Driving up to Georgian Bay and the weekend
cottage, my father on the crest
of each Hockley Hill: *Hold onto*

your tummies. We did. And were airborne.

Picture a single-stringed instrument for some
neglected god. Hermes, say, or Raven. He needs
to be Trickster, corvid. Make the string

sinew, come from flesh and the supple
memory of the body. The sounding-board
is rilled and pitted on the bottom but open-

ended and massive. Only a god
can play it. This is not a lyre; what we
are making here is sturdier —

call it resonance, call it time. Tune it as low
as you can, G below deepest A, more minor
than minor. Whisker in the dark. Wait for a fine

breath to set the whole in motion. Let wind
thrum as it will and watch the visible harmonics. Now
try to mute it.

What is the lifespan of a bridge? One November
the cold wind from Puget Sound turned
interrogative in the Narrows, pushed

and nuzzled, tickled the wires to hear
how they would sing — what tune, how high.
Four months old, the rolling deck fluttered in the wake

and added torsion to its dead load. In the film
of that day two lanes of traffic
stop. Drivers fall out of their cars

running, solid asphalt bounding underfoot
like the rapids they'd thought they could
avoid.

Jet stream, eddies, vapour trails. Ripples
and runnels — a scientist on the radio
talks turbulence, snaky air. He reminds us

we live in the depths of a fluid
world, a sea of currents, turmoil,
vortices — and we are

rocks in the stream, bottom-feeding bodies
immersed. Herakleion lost in
swirling silt. Blink, inhale, comb your hair

or stay perfectly still. Your being here
sends airplanes bucking, tips the ferry,
slings spirals down tornado alley.

Eighty beats per second.
What hurricane does this hummer
spawn, hovering at the feeder? Where will

the storm land? Who will we name it for?

As children we spun in circles on the lawn, arms
out like propeller blades, until the current
in our heads dropped us to the grass, laughing

at the tilt of the world. Sometimes the film
of the bridge is shown as comedy, for that same
seasick tumble. The bridge sways

like a three-a.m. drunk. "The Ups
and Downs of Bridges," one paper calls it. Or pride
before the fall. And fall it does: the cables

snap and the dead load collapses.
Luckily no one was hurt,
the narrator says. Let it

fall. The rubble is meaningless, it tells us only
that things end the way we expect. What keeps me
awake is the muscled animal

of ground ungrounded. The billowing deck
solid, then fluid, roiling. Something was given
body that day — not disaster

but its writhing entrance, its indifference.
How could anyone sleep, knowing this?
Hold onto your tummies.

      ↩

Which drink was my father's
last straw? What accident started
the tremors he couldn't control? At seventy

his brain turned chaotic, misfired. His barometer
dropped to Stormy and stayed there. He grew festinate
or the world too slow and sloping. By the time

of his last son's wedding Dad was glacial
and shivering, shrunk Parkinsonian
in his tux and waiting for the world

to end. Then someone played Glenn Miller, and he was
on the floor, the perfect sway and swing
of the forties, his forties, daughter-in-law spinning

in his arms. Some of us said he looked
like Fred Astaire. Then the record stopped.
In the video you can see him come alive

and die again, can follow the passage
of the eye of the storm. Here, let me
rewind it for you. *Begin the Beguine.*

This is getting out of hand. Listen:

the sky of my father's death was flat, cloudless,
sun-baked. The oceans of the world
were still. Miles up, passengers unbuckled

and reclined in their seats. No drinks
spilled. The wings of my heart
thumped on and on. An old man pushing

a wheelbarrow of flowers surprised me
on the street. *Beautiful day,* he said, *perfect.*
And I agreed. It was.

Crossing the Strait

Our wake takes in bay, holds
island & strait. This is how it looks

to move forward, the past growing behind us,
we could never dream how much. See what

we drag after us, contrails in time's element. We inhale
rain from Tokyo, exhale storms over Drumheller. This is all

I've ever tried to say: it's good to be here. Some days
that's not enough. We butt heads, drop forks,

forget how body enjoys body. The sleep we curve into
is the perfect shape of remembrance: O this is why

I'm here, this back, these arms. More sound,
less words. What I want. Rest on me. Let the ferry

shudder from crest to crest. Somewhere a bridge
collapses, something explodes. Let it. A man & woman

lean against plastic seats & are rocked to sleep.

Acknowledgements

I am grateful to the Canada Council for the Arts for its generous support during the writing of these poems.

Many of the poems in this collection first appeared in *Grain*, *Event*, *Pottersfield Portfolio*, *The Antigonish Review*, *The Fiddlehead* and *The Malahat Review*. "Drunk, with Axe" and "Burn Unit" were winners in *The Antigonish Review*'s Great Blue Heron poetry contest. "Parlez-moi d'amour" won *Pottersfield Portfolio*'s Compact Poetry Competition. My thanks to the editors of these journals.

The Writing Studio at the Banff Centre for the Arts provided space, time and much-needed companionship. My sincere thanks to the incredible staff at the Centre and to all the faculty and participants who made the Studio such a memorable experience. Particular thanks to Don McKay, Barry Dempster and Rachel Wyatt.

Rosana Roth offered long years of love, support and encouragement. Part one of this book is for her.

A deep bow to Sue Sinclair, my amazing editor, who came to this book with a sharp eye, an attentive ear and an expansive heart. A million thanks to everyone at Goose Lane Editions, especially Ross Leckie for his determined support of the manuscript, Lisa Rousseau for her wonderful design work, and Laurel Boone for keeping a steady hand on the tiller.

Jan Zwicky makes the world a better place. Peter Rist continues to be my best source of friendship and inspiration.

And Marlene Cookshaw rocks my world.

Mitchell Parry's professional interests are English literature and film studies, but his career has included brief stints as a lumber mill worker, a radio broadcaster, a teacher of ESL, and an arts administrator.

Many of the poems in *Tacoma Narrows* first appeared in *Grain*, *Event*, *The Fiddlehead* and *The Malahat Review*. "Drunk, with Axe" and "Burn Unit" won *The Antigonish Review*'s Great Blue Heron poetry contest, and "Parlez-moi d'amour" won *Pottersfield Portfolio*'s Compact Poetry Competition.

Mitchell Parry divides his time between Victoria, where he teaches at the University of Victoria, and Pender Island, where he lives as a gentleman farmer